D1409802

ROY HALLADAY

Tammy Gagne

Mitchell Lane

PUBLISHERS

P.O. Box 196
Hockessin, Delaware 19707
Visit us on the web: www.mitchelllane.com
Comments? email us: mitchelllane@mitchelllane.com

Printing   1   2   3   4   5   6   7   8   9

A Robbie Reader Biography

Library of Congress Cataloging-in-Publication Data
Gagne, Tammy.
 Roy Halladay / by Tammy Gagne.
   p. cm. — (A robbie reader)
 Includes bibliographical references and index.
 ISBN 978-1-61228-061-5 (library bound)
 1. Halladay, Roy, 1977-—Juvenile literature. 2. Baseball players—United States—Biography—Juvenile literature. 3. Pitchers (Baseball)—United States—Biography—Juvenile literature. I. Title.
 GV865.H233G34 2012
 796.357092—dc22
 [B]
                                                                 2011016786
eBook ISBN: 9781612281735

ABOUT THE AUTHOR: Tammy Gagne is the author of numerous books for adults and children, including My Guide to the Constitution: *The Power of the States* for Mitchell Lane Publishers. She resides in northern New England with her husband and son. One of her favorite pastimes is visiting schools to speak to kids about the writing process.

PUBLISHER'S NOTE: The following story has been thoroughly researched and to the best of our knowledge represents a true story. While every possible effort has been made to ensure accuracy, the publisher will not assume liability for damages caused by inaccuracies in the data, and makes no warranty on the accuracy of the information contained herein. This story has not been authorized or endorsed by Roy Halladay.

TABLE OF CONTENTS

Words in **bold** type can be found in the glossary.

On May 29, 2010, Roy Halladay pitched in a winning game against the Florida Marlins.

CHAPTER ONE

A Perfect Game

Phillies pitcher Roy Halladay was about to make May 29, 2010, go down in history. The ninth inning against the Florida Marlins had just begun, and he hadn't allowed a single player on base all night. Two pinch hitters, Mike Lamb and Wes Helms, had tried to get the job done. Both had failed. The crowd of Phillies fans was roaring. Now Florida's Ronny Paulino was stepping up to the plate. Unless he could break Halladay's rhythm, the Phillies pitcher would throw his first **perfect game.** Only 19 other players in the history of Major League Baseball had ever gone an entire game without allowing a single hit.

Halladay and teammates Ryan Howard (left) and Carlos Ruiz celebrate a perfect game in Miami, Florida.

Paulino hit the first pitch into the seats on the first-base side—a foul. Next came one ball and then one strike. When Roy threw his 115th pitch of the night, Paulino's bat made contact. He sent a ground ball to third, which Juan Castro promptly delivered to Ryan Howard at first base. Out! It was a perfect game!

Halladay smiled wide and hugged catcher Carlos Ruiz. The rest of the team mobbed them, shouting congratulations (kun-grah-choo-LAY-shuns).

Phillies manager Charlie Manuel had probably never been so happy about a 1-0 win. "He did what he had to do," he said after the game. "We gave him one run. He made it stand up."

According to the *Huffington Post,* Roy said he thought he had a chance once he got the first two outs in the ninth. "You're always aware of [the possibility]," he said. "[But] it's not something that you expect."

Roy has always been one to shoot for the stars, but he is no stranger to defeat.

Halladay has amazing concentration when he is pitching. He says that he goes into "isolation mode" at this time. He tries to plan every pitch and won't talk to anyone but his manager and pitching coach. He won't talk to teammates, reporters, or fans until he has finished pitching a game.

The Great American Pastime

Harry Leroy Halladay III was born on May 14, 1977. The nickname Roy is from his middle name. His parents, Harry Jr. and Linda, had three children in all. Roy has an older sister named Merinda and a younger sister named Heather. The three siblings grew up in Arvada, Colorado—a **suburb** of Denver.

Like many American kids, Roy discovered baseball as a young boy. He and his father began tossing a ball around when Roy was just three years old. At five he joined a T-ball team. His father even built a batting cage and pitcher's mound in the family's basement so that Roy could practice when it was too cold to play outdoors.

Roy speaks proudly of his father. He told *Sports Illustrated,* "My dad played high school baseball. But the biggest thing I got from him was his approach to life. We were always going to do something productive, always go the extra mile. The extra things that were done, that's what separates people."

Roy loved playing baseball, and he was very good at it. Many people thought he was a natural athlete. He was strong, tall, and extremely skilled for such a young person.

His biggest shortcoming was his temper. When he focused on the game, no one could beat him. When he got angry, he did not do well on the field.

Roy tried different positions to see which one fit him best. As soon as he stepped onto the pitcher's mound, he knew he belonged there. At just 14, some very important people noticed his pitching talent. Major league **scouts** were coming to watch him play. One scout, Bus Campbell, began working with Roy one on one.

Roy called Bus Campbell (inset) his second grandfather. "The old man loved working with young pitchers and never took a dime for the countless hours he gave them. I'd go see him once or twice a week," he said. "He almost became part of our family. It was just a special relationship." Halladay often passes along some of what he learned from Bus to younger pitchers on the Phillies, like Cole Hamels (right).

Halladay showed his famous intensity during spring training in 1999, when he was 22 years old and ready to prove what he could do.

To the Majors and Back

Roy graduated from Arvada West High School in 1995. Shortly afterward, the Toronto Blue Jays picked him in the **amateur** (AM-ih-chur) draft. He played in the minors until he made the major league team in 1998.

At 6 feet, 6 inches tall, he stood out right away. His skills were even more impressive than his height, though. In his second game, against the Detroit Tigers, Halladay nearly pitched a **no-hitter.** Only one other Blue Jays player, Dave Stieb, had ever thrown a no-hitter. Halladay's major league career was off to an excellent start.

Roy pitched in 36 games during 1999. He was the starting pitcher in 18 of them. In May of that year, he pitched a complete **shutout** in another game against the Tigers. He had a respectable **earned run average** (ERA) of 3.92.

The next two years were far less promising. Roy began allowing more and more hits. Soon his ERA had risen to 10.64. In 2001, he was sent back to the minor league team to work on his skills.

Being sent back to the minor league after making it to the majors had to be tough on Roy. He didn't let it destroy him, though. Instead, he used it as a chance to improve his skills.

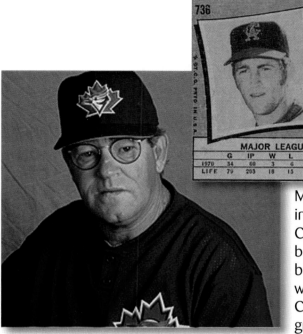

736
MEL QUEEN
CALIFORNIA ANGELS   PITCHER
Ht: 6'1"   Wt: 197   Throws: Right
Bats: Left Born: 3-26-42
Home: Morro Bay, Calif.

Originally an outfielder, Mel was used as a pinch-hitter, 10-1-70, & delivered an RBI Single in 13th inning to win final game of year for Angels vs. Chisox, 5-4. His father hurled for Yanks & Bucs, 1942-1952.

FIRST YEAR IN PRO BALL —1960
FIRST GAME IN MAJORS —1964

MAJOR LEAGUE PITCHING RECORD

	G	IP	W	L	PCT.	H	R	ER	SO	BB	ERA
1970	34	60	3	6	.333	58	28	28	44	28	4.20
LIFE	79	293	18	15	.545	256	128	108	234	95	3.32

Mel Queen believed in Roy. "Don't worry, Cy," he said. "You'll be back in the majors before you know it." He was comparing Roy to Cy Young, one of the greatest pitchers of all time.

Pitching coach Mel Queen helped him figure out his problem. He thought Roy was relying on his strength too much. Together they worked on making Roy's pitching **technique** (tek-NEEK) better.

Roy also realized that he was letting his emotions get the better of him again. When the pressure was on, he would overthrow. He learned to put his energy into clever throwing instead of fast pitching alone. This change made all the difference. He returned to the majors before the end of the season.

When Halladay learned how to balance strength and technique, he was back in the majors.

Rookie No More

Back on the major league team, Halladay's career kept getting hotter. He was the starting pitcher in 16 games. He ended the 2001 season with a 5-3 record and an ERA of 3.19.

At some point people began calling him Doc Halladay. The nickname refers to a Wild West gunslinger who had an incredibly fast arm. The Wild West Doc Holliday was known for being fast with a pistol. The pitcher Doc Halladay is known for being fast with a baseball. He can throw a ball 95 miles per hour.

Between 2002 and 2010, Roy played in seven All-Star games. He was scheduled to play in an eighth, in 2005, but was injured. A **line**

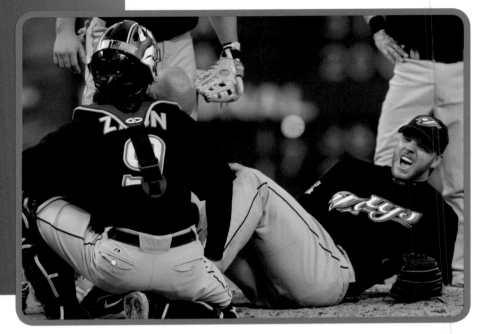

Catcher Gregg Zaun checks out Roy's broken shin in the July 18, 2005, game against the Texas Rangers.

drive by Kevin Mench of the Texas Rangers drilled Roy's leg and broke it. The injury ended his 2005 season.

The Blue Jays named Roy their Pitcher of the Year every single year from 2005 to 2009. He had clearly earned his teammates' respect. B.J. Ryan told the *Sporting News* that the first thing he noticed when he joined the Blue Jays was what a hard worker Roy was. "He was at our spring training facility weeks before camp started. And once the rest of the guys were there, they'd start rolling in at around 9:30 most mornings—but Doc was there at 7."

Roy was **traded** to the Philadelphia Phillies after the 2009 season. Although Philadelphia was thrilled to get him, his Toronto fans were disappointed. Roy bought a full-page ad in the *Toronto Sun* newspaper to thank them and the city for the great time he'd had there. He was moving on, but he was sad, too.

Roy and his wife Brandy on the day he joined the Phillies. The couple have known each other since they were children. Brandy moved away when she was around 12. When she returned to the Denver area at age 22, they ran into each other at a gym and began dating shortly after.

19

	1	2	3	4	5	6	7	8	9		R	H
CIN	0	0	0	0	0	0	0	0			0	0
PHI	1	3	0	0	0	0	0	0			4	5

**Halladay pitches in the ninth inning
of his no-hitter against the Reds.**

Like everything else, though, Roy gave the move his all. His pitching coach, Rich Dubee, said, "There's always something he's trying to do to get better. That's the amazing thing. He's . . . always trying to improve his game."

Roy started this new chapter with his biggest milestone yet. His May 2010 perfect game against the Florida Marlins made major league history.

The Phillies reached the playoffs that year, and in the first game against the Cincinnati Reds, Halladay made history again. He pitched a no-hitter, walking just one batter. It was only the second postseason no-hitter in baseball history. Counted with the perfect game, Halladay became just the fifth player in history to pitch two no-hitters in one season.

Halladay has won the Cy Young Award, one of the most impressive pitching awards, twice. His first win was in 2003 when he was still with Toronto. The second time was his first year with Philadelphia.

Roy with Braden (center), Brandy, and Ryan. Roy is well known for being a true family man. He once turned down an offer to be on *Late Night With David Letterman* because it was Ryan's sixth birthday.

An Ace

Between baseball seasons, Roy and his family live in Odessa, Florida. He and his wife, Brandy, have two sons, Braden and Ryan.

In his spare time, Roy enjoys fishing. Shortly after his perfect game in 2010, his teammates gave him a special gift. They arranged for him to go bass fishing with Skeet Reese, a famous **angler.** Roy's sons joined them on the trip.

One of the best parts of being a successful Major League Baseball player is being able to give something back through charity. When Roy was playing for the Blue Jays, he

Roy sets aside time to meet with special fans, like these kids from the Isaac Foundation. In 2008, he was named The George Gross/Toronto Sun Sportsperson of the Year. He donated the award money to the foundation.

and Brandy started Doc's Box. The program worked with Ronald McDonald House and local children's hospitals. The Halladays invited 10 to 15 children and their families to watch home games from a fancy suite, or box, in the stadium.

Roy has also worked with the Make-A-Wish Foundation. He finds it humbling when an ill child's biggest wish is to meet him. "It's definitely a tremendous honor to have somebody want that," he told the foundation.

As part of his contract with the Blue Jays, Roy also donated $100,000 of his salary each year to the Jays Care Foundation. This charity works with **underprivileged** children. It promotes health and education and teaches life skills. Brandy speaks highly of the program. She told the *Toronto Star,* "These [players] are interested in the community. I think it's cool that the team supports that."

Roy's career hasn't always been easy, but that is part of why he is such a great role model. His ups and downs—and more ups— show just what a person can do by never giving

up. Roy told *Sporting News,* "I can handle the boos. But if I look in the mirror and know I didn't give it my all, that's more disappointing."

Phillies fans have high hopes for the future, and Roy is a big part of the reason. When Cliff Lee was added to the Phillies **roster** in December 2010, Roy became part of the

Philadelphia's four aces (left to right): Cole Hamels, Cliff Lee, Roy Oswalt, and Roy Halladay

Phillies four aces. This skilled group of pitchers also includes Cole Hamels and Roy Oswalt. Many fans were thinking the foursome just might lead the Phillies to another World Series title. By the end of June 2011, Halladay was helping that happen. He was leading the National League in wins and strikeouts.

27

CHRONOLOGY

1977 Harry Leroy "Roy" Halladay III is born on May 14 in Denver, Colorado.

1991 Roy begins working with pitching coach Bus Campbell.

1995 He graduates from Arvada West High School. The Toronto Blue Jays pick him in their amateur draft.

1998 He moves up to the Toronto Blue Jays major league team. In his second game, he nearly pitches a no-hitter, with Bobby Higginson's home run the only hit granted.

1999 He pitches a shutout game against the Detroit Tigers on May 20.

2000 His son Braden is born.

2001 After a pitching slump, Halladay is sent back to the minor league, but returns to the majors before the end of the season.

2002 He plays in his first All-Star game.

2003 He receives his first Cy Young Award.

2004 His son Ryan is born.

2005 A line drive breaks Roy's leg. Even though he is out for the rest of the season, Toronto teammates vote him Pitcher of the Year.

2006 He signs a three-year extension with Toronto for $40 million.

2007 He and the Blue Jays beat the Chicago White Sox for Halladay's 100th career win.

2008 Halladay loses three complete games in a row for Toronto. The last Blue Jays pitcher to do this was Jim Clancy in 1982.

2009 His 1.3 walks per nine innings pitched is the lowest in the American League. At the end of the season, Halladay is traded to the Philadelphia Phillies.

2010 On May 29, he pitches the 20th perfect game in history. On October 6, he pitches the first postseason no-hitter since 1956. He receives his second Cy Young Award. When the Phillies sign Cliff Lee, Halliday becomes part of a four-player pitching powerhouse.

2011 On April 13, he pitches a shutout until the first out of the ninth inning. Eleven days later, he ties his career high of strikeouts in a game when he fans 14 San Diego Padres. In the middle of June, the Phillies pitching staff leads the league with lowest ERA.

CAREER STATISTICS

Year	Team	GS	W	L	IP	H	ER	HR	BB	CG	K	ERA
1998	Blue Jays	2	1	0	14.0	9	3	2	2	1	13	1.93
1999	Blue Jays	18	8	7	149.1	156	65	19	79	1	82	3.92
2000	Blue Jays	13	4	7	67.2	107	80	14	42	0	44	10.64
2001	Blue Jays	16	5	3	105.1	97	37	3	25	1	96	3.16
2002	Blue Jays	34	19	7	239.1	223	78	10	62	2	168	2.93
2003	Blue Jays	36	22	7	266.0	253	96	26	32	9	204	3.25
2004	Blue Jays	21	8	8	133.0	140	62	13	39	1	95	4.20
2005	Blue Jays	19	12	4	141.2	118	38	11	18	5	108	2.41
2006	Blue Jays	32	16	5	220.0	208	78	19	34	4	132	3.19
2007	Blue Jays	31	16	7	225.1	232	93	15	48	7	139	3.71
2008	Blue Jays	33	20	11	246.0	220	76	18	39	9	206	2.78
2009	Blue Jays	32	17	10	239.0	234	74	22	35	9	208	2.79
2010	Phillies	33	21	10	250.2	231	68	24	30	9	219	2.44
Career		320	169	86	2297.1	2228	848	196	485	58	1714	3.64

GS = Games Started, W = Wins, L = Losses, IP = Innings Pitched, H = Hits, ER = Earned Runs, HR = Home Runs Allowed, BB = Bases on Balls, CG = Complete Games, K = Strikeouts, ERA = Earned Run Average

FIND OUT MORE

Books

Jackson, Dave. *Philadelphia Phillies.* San Diego, California: Sportszone, 2011.

"Pitchers Rule: Roy Halladay, Josh Johnson, Ubaldo Jimenez." *Sports Illustrated,* July 5, 2010.

Savage, Jeff. *Roy Halladay.* Minneapolis: Lerner, 2011.

Works Consulted

Associated Press. "Roy Halladay Thanks Toronto Fans With Newspaper Ad." *NESN,* December 22, 2009. http://www.nesn.com/2009/12/roy-halladay-thanks-toronto-fans-with-newspaper-ad.html

"Back in Time: March 16, 2006." *Sports Illustrated Vault.* http://sportsillustrated.cnn.com/vault/gallery/featured/GAL1153234/5/6/index.htm

Beam, Matt. "Arm Force: Roy Halladay." *Toronto Life,* July, 2004.

Elliott, Bob. "Family Cheers on Roy Halladay." *Toronto Sun,* October 11, 2010.

———. "Halladay's Sons Get Their Trip." *Toronto Sun,* July 6, 2009.

Greenberg, Steve. "I Have a Window of Opportunity That's Getting Smaller." *Sporting News,* February 15, 2010.

FIND OUT MORE

Griffin, Richard. "Halladays Step Up to the Plate to Help Others."
    The [Toronto] Star, June 14, 2008. http://www.thestar.com/
    Sports/Baseball/article/443398

Krasovic, Tom. "Roy Halladay Throws No-Hitter Against Reds to Open
    Playoffs." *AOL News,* October 6, 2010.http://www.aolnews.
    com/2010/10/06/roy-halladay-throws-no-hitter-against-reds-to-
    open-playoffs/

McCarron, Anthony. "Timeline: Career Highlights—and Lowlights—of
    Ace Roy Halladay, Reportedly Set to Join Phillies." *New York Daily
    News,* December 15, 2009.

Ortiz, Jorge L. "Phillies Halladay Wins Second Cy Young." *USA Today,*
    November 17, 2010.

O'Sullivan, Dan. "Cy Young Roy Halladay Meets Ex-AOY." *Bassmaster,—*
    December 8, 2010. http://sports.espn.go.com/outdoors/
    bassmaster/news/story?id=5872451

Reynolds, Tim. "Roy Halladay PERFECT GAME: Philly Throws
    20th in MLB History." *Huffington Post,* May 29, 2010. http://
    www.huffingtonpost.com/2010/05/29/roy-halladay-perfect-
    game_n_594598.html

Sandler, Jeremy. "A Special Halladay." Make-A-Wish Canada, reprinted
    from Dunedin, Florida, *National Post,* n.d. http://www.makeawish.
    ca/news_and_media/news/read/971

Schonbrun, Zach. "Ceremony Honors Halladay's Perfecto."
    MLB.com, June 5, 2010. http://mlb.mlb.com/news/article.
    jsp?c_id=mlb&content_id=10837954&fext=.jsp&notebook_
    id=10839196&vkey=notebook_mlb&ymd=20100605

Verducci, Tom. "What Makes Roy Run." *Sports Illustrated,* April 5, 2010.

On the Internet

MLB.com: Roy Halladay
    http://mlb.mlb.com/team/player.jsp?player_id=136880

Official Site of the Philadelphia Phillies
    http://philadelphia.phillies.mlb.com/index.jsp?c_id=phi

Sports Illustrated Kids
    http://www.sikids.com/

GLOSSARY

amateur (AM-ih-chur)—A person who plays a sport for enjoyment and not for pay.

angler (ANG-ler)—A person who fishes with a hook and line.

earned run average (URND RUN AV-rij)—The total number of runs a pitcher gives up divided by the number of innings pitched, then multiplied by 9. This gives the number of runs the pitcher gives up, on average, for every nine-inning baseball game pitched. (Runs scored as a result of errors are not counted in this number.)

line drive—A ball that is hit in a straight line, with very little height.

no-hitter (noh-HIT-er)—A baseball game in which a pitcher gives up no hits (although players may have gotten on base as a result of errors or walks).

perfect game (PUR-fekt GAYM)—A baseball game in which a pitcher allows no players on base.

roster (RAH-ster)—The list of players on a team.

scout—A person whose job is to look for talented young athletes to sign up for a particular sports team.

shutout (SHUT-out)—Any game in which the opposing team does not score.

suburb (SUB-urb)—A community of homes just outside a city.

technique (tek-NEEK)—The way in which an athlete performs the skills of a sport.

trade (TRAYD)—An exchange of baseball players between teams.

underprivileged (un-der-PRIV-lijd)—Denied a benefit because of lack of money or other circumstances.

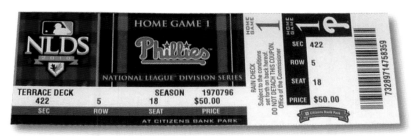

INDEX